YOUR LIGHT HAS COME

Inspirational guidelines
to help you cope with today
and anticipate tomorrow

by
Nathanael Olson

First Printing

Editorial Director, James Kuse
Managing Editor, Ralph Luedtke
Production Editor/Manager, Richard Lawson
Photographic Editor, Gerald Koser

designed by

Marty Zens

COPYRIGHT © 1978 BY IDEALS PUBLISHING CORPORATION
MILWAUKEE, WIS. 53201
ALL RIGHTS RESERVED. PRINTED AND BOUND IN U.S.A.

ISBN 0-89542-574-2 150

CONTENTS

LIGHT AND HOPE 5

My New Mission 11

LIGHT FOR YOUR PRESENT ... 15

The Bible—
   A Blueprint for Good Living 16

How to Know What to Do 40

God Created the Material World 63

LIGHT FOR YOUR FUTURE 75

The Best Is Yet to Come 78

LIGHT AND HOPE

"Arise, shine, for thy light is come . . ."

(Isa. 60:1)

The Pointed Question Winston Churchill Asked Billy Graham . . .

In 1954, when Billy Graham visited Sir Winston Churchill at 10 Downing Street, he found the famed statesman hunched over a table. Suddenly, Churchill looked up, and with earnestness written on his face asked the American evangelist, "Young man, do you have any hope?"

A quarter of a century has slipped by since then and desperate people everywhere are asking the same question, "Is there any hope?"

Surely any thinking person would have to confess that the light of any earthly hope is getting dimmer with each passing year. Man's inhumanity to man is increasing, not decreasing.

We must look up to God if we are to find hope, faith, and love—the intangibles which make life worth living.

When Debby Boone was interviewed about her hit record, "You Light Up My Life," she revealed the reason she was able to throw her soul into this song—to her it was a prayer song to God, the one who lights up her life with the glory of his presence.

In the pages that follow, you will discover warm, solid reasons for facing today and tomorrow with confidence.

You don't have to be afraid of the dark. "Your light has come!"

The Bible—An Unfailing Source of Light

A.Z. Conrad

Jesus said, "Heaven and earth shall pass away but my words shall not pass away" (Matt. 24:35).

Century follows century. *There it stands.*
Empires rise and fall and are forgotten. *There it stands.*
Dynasty succeeds dynasty. *There it stands.*
Kings are crowned and uncrowned. *There it stands.*
Emperors decree its extermination. *There it stands.*
Storms of hate swirl about it. *There it stands.*
Atheists rail against it. *There it stands.*
Unbelief abandons it. *There it stands.*
Thunderbolts of wrath smite it. *There it stands.*
An anvil that has broken a million hammers. *There it stands.*
The flames are kindled about it. *There it stands.*
The tooth of time gnaws but dents it not. *There it stands.*
Infidels predict its abandonment. *There it stands.*
Devotees of folly denounce it. *There it stands.*

It is God's highway to Paradise.
It is the light on the pathway in the darkest night.
It leads businessmen to integrity and uprightness.
It is the great consoler in bereavement.
It awakens men and women opiated by sin.
It answers every great question of the soul.
It solves every great problem of life.
It is a fortress often attacked but never failing.
Its wisdom is commanding and its logic convincing.
Salvation is its watchword. Eternal life its goal.
It punctures all pretense.
It is forward-looking, outward-looking, and upward-looking.
It outlives, outlifts, outloves, outreaches, outranks, outruns all other books.

Trust it, love it, obey it and eternal life is yours.

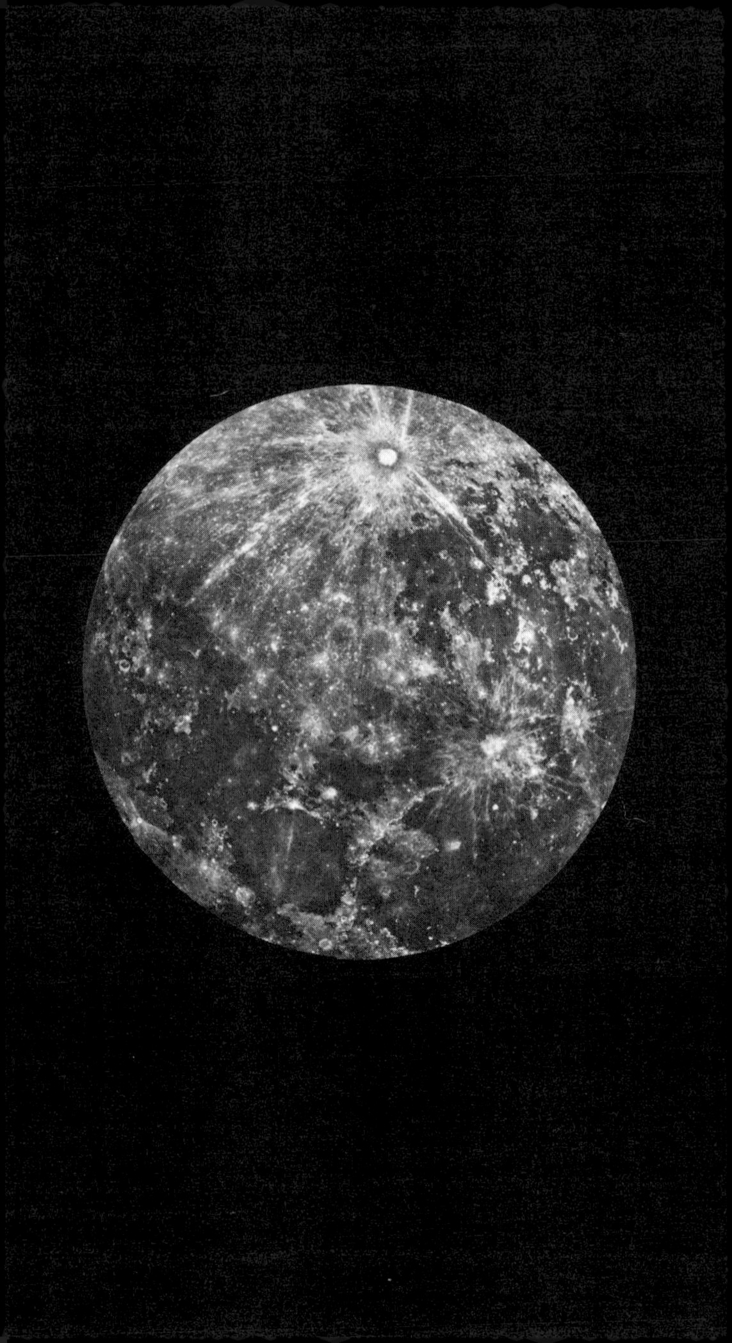

My New Mission

Colonel James B. Irwin, Astronaut

I trained for five years in preparation for my trip to the moon. There were many times when I asked the question, "Will I ever be able to learn everything necessary for this mission?" I daily asked God for guidance during this preparation—a preparation of body, mind, and spirit. At last, on 26 July 1971 we blasted off the pad, slipped the "surly bonds of earth" and soared into space to begin the history-making mission of Apollo 15.

The flight was an experience that was to transform my life—an experience that almost boggles the mind when one tries to describe the inner feelings. The senses are stirred by the things one sees with the eyes, and feels inside. The picture of the earth—our home, the blue planet—hanging in the blackness of space was a sight to behold. It truly looked like a Christmas tree ornament because we could not see the fragile band of atmosphere that surrounds the earth. We were stunned by the beauty of our home, and convinced that it is unique and truly the only home for man.

On the surface of the moon, I was awed by the majesty of the Appenine Mountains. I was touched by the hand of God. He was there to answer my prayers, guide us to the white Genesis rock, and inspire me to quote the 121st Psalm. It was the greatest experience of my life—to travel to the moon and find God there to answer all our needs.

I believe that God allowed me to travel to the moon and look to the earth so that I could share His greatness and the smallness—yet uniqueness—of man. Yes, God loves all of us so much that He sent His Son to the spaceship earth to give us all a mission in life.

The most satisfying moment in my life was the time at the age of eleven when I invited Jesus into my life. I hope to share my "discoveries" with all people on the earth. High Flight's purpose is to insure that people enjoy a higher way of life—and in the final stage that will insure that we are ready for the ultimate flight, beyond the moon into the glory of heaven.

I will lift up mine eyes unto the hills, from whence cometh my help.

My help cometh from the Lord, which made heaven and earth.

He will not suffer thy foot to be moved: he that keepeth thee will not slumber.

Behold, he that keepeth Israel shall neither slumber nor sleep.

The Lord is thy keeper: the Lord is thy shade upon thy right hand.

The sun shall not smite thee by day, nor the moon by night.

The Lord shall preserve thee from all evil: he shall preserve thy soul.

The Lord shall preserve thy going out and thy coming in from this time forth, and even for evermore.

Psalm 121

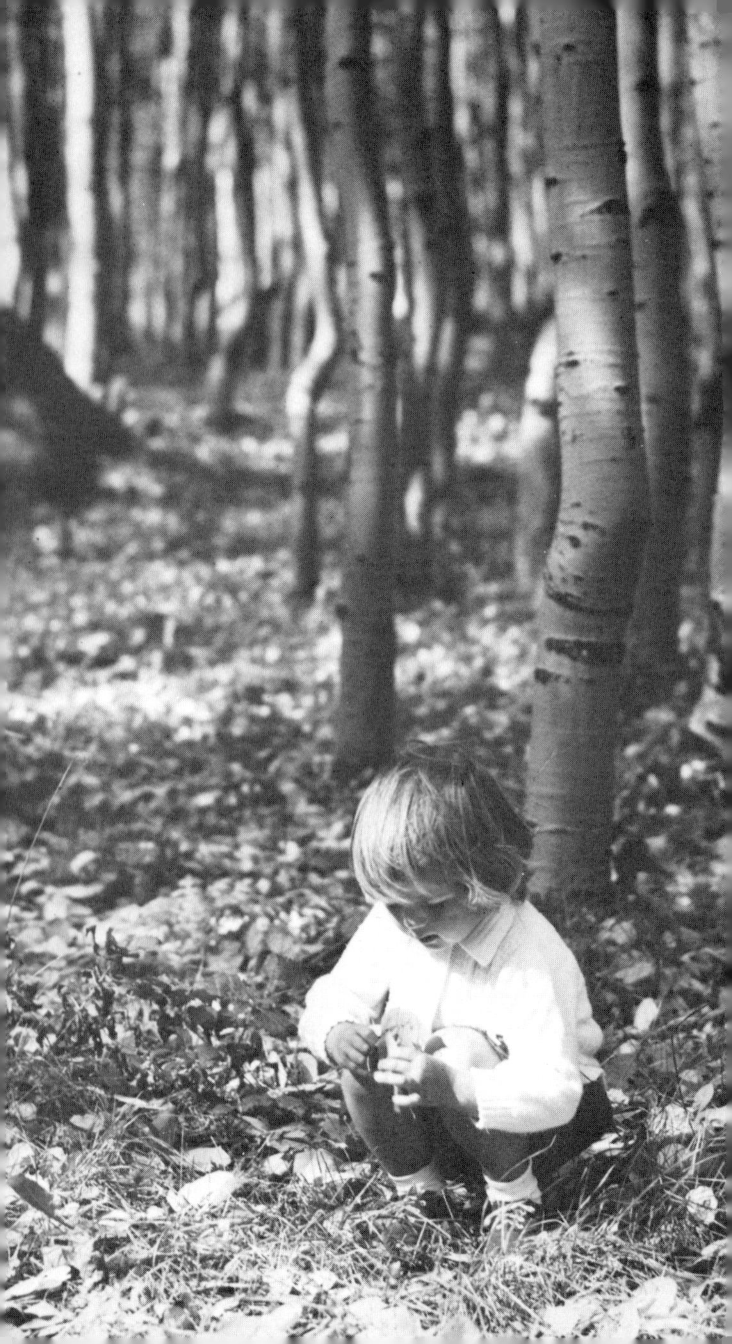

LIGHT FOR YOUR PRESENT

My God shall supply all your needs according to his riches in glory by Christ Jesus.

(Phil. 4:19)

The Bible — A Blueprint for Good Living

When asked if he read the Bible, the famed psychiatrist Dr. Smiley Blanton replied, "I not only read it, I study it. It's the greatest textbook on human behavior ever put together. If people could just absorb its message, a lot of us psychiatrists could close our offices and go fishing."

Later, Dr. Blanton pointed out that it is foolish to neglect the Bible in which is recorded 3,000 years of distilled wisdom.

The following verses are just a sampling of "God's psychiatry":

PEACE

"Thou wilt keep him in perfect peace, whose mind is stayed on thee: because he trusteth in thee" (Is. 26:3).

STRENGTH

"They that wait upon the Lord shall renew their strength" (Is. 40:31).

SUCCESS

"This book of the law shall not depart out of thy mouth . . . then thou shalt have good success" (Josh. 1:8).

Psalm 37:5 gives two commands and one promise: "Commit thy way unto the Lord; trust also in him, and he shall bring it to pass."

This is a psychologically sound principle. Set goals and then move toward them confidently, without anxious effort. "Lean not unto thine own understanding" (Prov. 3:5).

HEALTH

Moses told the Israelites the Lord God had promised them that if they would keep his statutes, He would not put any of the diseases upon them which had come upon the Egyptians (Exod. 15:26).

The lifestyle of the believer should be freer from stress than the life of the unbeliever; therefore, the believer can expect to escape many of the afflictions that plague today's generation.

Standing on the Promises

Everek R. Storms

The Holy Scriptures contain a total of 8,810 promises. How do I know? I counted them.

All my life I have seen various figures quoted as to the number of promises in the Bible; the one most generally given being 30,000.

Since this is a round number with four zeros to it, I have always been a little suspicious about it. Furthermore, since there are only 31,101 verses in the Bible, it would mean that there would be practically one promise for every verse.

I do not guarantee my count to be perfect, but it is the most accurate I know of.

The Bible contains eight kinds of promises. There are 7,487 promises that God has given to man. This is about 85 percent of all the promises in the Bible.

There are almost 1,000 instances recorded—991 to be exact—in which one person makes a promise to another person. This is some 11 percent of all the promises in the Scriptures. An example is the promise made by the Chaldeans to King Nebuchadnezzar: "Let the king tell his servants the dream, and we will shew the interpretation of it" (Dan. 2:7).

There are also 290 promises made by man to God. The majority of these—235 of them—are to be found in the Psalms, such as, "O Lord, open thou my lips; and my mouth shall shew forth thy praise" (51:15).

There are twenty-eight promises that were made by angels. Most of these—twenty-three of them—are found in Luke. One example is the promise made by the angel to the women at Jesus' tomb: "Behold, he goeth before you into Galilee; there shall ye see him" (Matt. 28:7).

There are actually nine promises made by that old liar, the devil, e.g., "All these things will I give thee, if thou wilt fall down and worship me" (Matt. 4:9).

Two promises were made by an evil spirit. "Then there came out a spirit, and stood before the Lord, and said, I will entice him" (2 Chron. 18:20).

There are also two promises made by God the Father to God the Son, and one made by a man to an angel.

One of the sixty-six books of the Bible has no promises at all—Titus. Seventeen others contain less than ten promises each. Even such an outstanding book as Ephesians has only six promises.

The question as to which are the greatest promises is one about which there would be a difference of opinion. But if I were permitted to claim only six promises, I would choose the following:

The promise of salvation: "If thou shalt confess with thy mouth the Lord Jesus, and shalt believe in thine heart that God hath raised him from the dead, thou shalt be saved" (Rom. 10:9).

The promise of the Holy Spirit: "Ye shall receive power, after that the Holy Ghost is come upon you" (Acts 1:8).

The promise of answered prayer: "If ye abide in me, and my words abide in you, ye shall ask what ye will, and it shall be done unto you" (John 15:7).

The promise of temporal help: "Seek ye first the kingdom of God, and his righteousness; and all these things shall be added unto you" (Matt. 6:33).

The promise of sustaining strength: "As thy days, so shall thy strength be" (Deut. 33:25).

The promise of heaven: "If I go and prepare a place for you, I will come again, and receive you unto myself; that where I am, there ye may be also" (John 14:3).

Yes, God promises to save and sanctify us, hear us when we pray, provide us with food and clothing, give us enough strength for each day, and eventually take us to heaven. What more can we want? If we had no other promises than these six, how good God would be to us!

The promises are ours for the asking —7,487 of them made by God Himself. They are waiting for us to test and prove them. We go to church and sing, "Standing on the promises," but most of us are simply sitting on them!

These are perilous times in which we are living. Recent developments in many lands emphasize this only too clearly. But the reply that Judson gave his mission board when they inquired about the prospects for the future in Burma is still true for all of us: "The future is as bright as the promises of God."

You can count on the promises of God. Why not try some of them and see for yourself?

<small>Used by permission of The Sower magazine, World Home Bible League</small>

A Vision of the King Through the Bible

Billy Sunday

Twenty-two years ago, with the Holy Spirit as my guide, I entered this wonderful temple called Christianity.

I entered at the portico of Genesis, walked down through the Old Testament art gallery where the pictures of Noah, Abraham, Moses, Joseph, Isaac, Jacob, and Daniel hang on the wall. I passed into the music room of the Psalms, where the spirit swept the keyboard of nature and brought forth the dirge-like wail of the weeping prophet Jeremiah, to the grand impassioned strain of Isaiah, until it seemed that every reed and pipe in God's great organ of nature responded to the tuneful harp of David, the sweet singer of Israel. I entered the chapel of Ecclesiastes where the voice of the preacher was heard, and into the conservatory where the Rose of Sharon and the Lily of the Valley's sweet-scented spices filled and perfumed my life. I entered the business office of Proverbs, then into the observatory room of the prophets where I saw telescopes of various sizes, some pointing to far-off events, but all concentrated upon the Bright and Morning Star which was to rise above the moonlight of Judea for our salvation.

I entered the audience room of the King of kings, and caught a vision of his glory from the standpoint of Matthew, Mark, Luke, and John; and passed into the Acts of the Apostles where the Holy Spirit was doing his work in the formation of the infant Church. Then into the correspondence room, where sat Matthew, Mark, Luke, John, Paul, Peter, James, and Jude, penning their epistles. I stepped into the throne room of Revelation where all towered into glittering peaks; and I had a vision of the King sitting upon his throne in all his glory — and I cried:

> All hail the power of Jesus' name,
> Let angels prostrate fall;
> Bring forth the royal diadem,
> And crown Him Lord of all!

Three Keys to Daily Joy

Key One

Each day, let God say something to you. Jesus said, "If ye abide in me, and my *words abide in you,* ye shall ask what ye will, and it shall be done unto you" (John 15:7).

There is no substitute for daily Bible reading. Therefore, study God's Word. Digest it. Meditate on it until your thoughts and emotions are filled with the word of God.

Key Two

Each day, you say something to God. Prayer is to the spirit what air is to the body. Jesus taught that men ought "always to pray, and not to faint" (Luke 18:1).

Learn to talk to God fervently, regularly, conversationally. "Ye have not, because ye ask not" (James 4:2). Ask God to fulfill your wants and needs so that he can shower bountiful blessings on you.

Key Three

Each day, say something about God to somebody else. Acts 1:8 teaches that we are to be "witnesses" of the Lord. A witness is a person who tells what he has seen and what he has heard. In other words, he is a sharer of his experiences.

When God blesses you, don't keep the good news to yourself, pass it on.

Use these three keys on a daily basis. Discover the wonderful way they open the doors to daily joy.

How to Cope with Your Fears

Writing to Timothy, the Apostle Paul declared, "God hath not given us the spirit of fear, but of power; and of love, and of a sound mind" (2 Tim. 1:7).

Napoleon Hill lists man's six basic fears as follows:

> The fear of failure
> The fear of criticism
> The fear of poverty
> The fear of loss of love
> The fear of old age
> The fear of death

The truly committed Christian need not give in to any of these fears. When he is a part of God's perfect will, there is no lasting failure. The sting of criticism is lessened by knowing that the Lord is our judge, not man. The fear of poverty disappears when God is trusted as the Total Source and the believer stands upon the promise, "Give, and it shall be given unto you" (Luke 6:38).

When earthly loves fail, the Christian still has "a friend that sticketh closer than a brother" (Prov. 18:24).

When silver threads appear among the gold, the believer knows he is that much nearer to his heavenly home and that the best is yet to be. And when he faces death, he does not face it alone. "I will fear no evil: for thou art with me . . ." (Ps. 23:4). Death is described as "the valley of the shadow of death" (Ps. 23:4). A shadow comes when an object gets between us and the sun. On the other side of that object is light. On the other side of death is a bright eternity with God.

In 1 John 4:18 we read, "There is no fear in love; but perfect love casteth out fear: because fear hath torment. He that feareth is not made perfect in love."

"God is love," perfect love (1 John 4:16). The more of Him we have in our minds and hearts, the less fear we will feel.

How to Enjoy Mental Health

The pages of the New Testament give us closeups of two great minds: Christ's and Paul's.

Philippians 2:5 exhorts, "Let this mind be in you, which was also in Christ Jesus." Verse 8 lists the two qualities of Christ's mind — humility and obedience. Wouldn't most of our problems be solved if humility, not pride, was uppermost? If obedience, rather than self-will, was our hallmark?

The fourth chapter of Luke gives us the scriptural way to resist temptation. When Satan tempted the Lord, Jesus answered his half-truths with whole truths. We must use the same rebuttal. Satan is "the accuser of our brethren" (Rev. 12:10). We must answer him with, "It is written." He fears the whole truth of God's Word.

Martin Luther, when reminded by Satan of all his sins, boldly declared: "The blood of Jesus Christ God's Son cleanses me from all sin."

In the parable of the Sower and the Seed (Matt. 13), Jesus listed two attitudes that destroy the effectiveness of the Word:

1) The cares of this life — draining our emotional/spiritual energy,

2) The deceitfulness of riches — building our hopes on money, not the Master.

Look at the lifestyle of Jesus and see how free He was from both attitudes!

The Apostle Paul's mind was also liberated from earthly bondage. That's why he could urge others: "If ye then be risen with Christ, seek those things which are above . . . Set your affection on things above, not on things on the earth" (Col. 3:1,2).

On the door of a humble shoe repair shop on a typical dirty city street, hung this sign, "Living Above." In other words, the shoemaker couldn't help where he made a living, but he could choose where to live. He was living upstairs — above the dirt and din of the city. We too are *in this world* but are not to be *of this world.*

What was the secret behind the Apostle Paul's good mental health? He kept his mind renewed. In Romans 12:2, he wrote, "Be not conformed to this world: but be ye transformed by the renewing of your mind . . ." If the mind is not transformed by daily renewal, it will become conformed, squeezed into a mold.

In 2 Timothy 4:13, Paul asks Timothy to make sure that he brings him his cloak, his books, but especially the parchments. Even at the close of his life and ministry, Paul was renewing his mind through the reading of the sacred parchments.

When he wrote to the church at Philippi, he told them to think on only things that are true, honest, just, pure, lovely, of good report, virtuous, and praiseworthy. Philippians 4:9 promises that if these things constitute our mental diet, "the God of peace shall be with you."

We are responsible for what we think.

Lincoln's Advice on Bible Reading

In 1864, Abraham Lincoln said to his friend, Joshua Speed: "Take all of this book [the Bible] upon reason that you can, and the balance on faith, and you will live and die a better man."

No mortal man can fully understand the immortal mind of Jehovah. "For my thoughts are not your thoughts, neither are your ways my ways, saith the Lord. For as the heavens are higher than the earth, so are my ways higher than your ways, and my thoughts than your thoughts" (Is. 55:8-9).

Believe God for what you do understand; trust Him for what you do not understand. This combination is the secret to enjoying God and His Word.

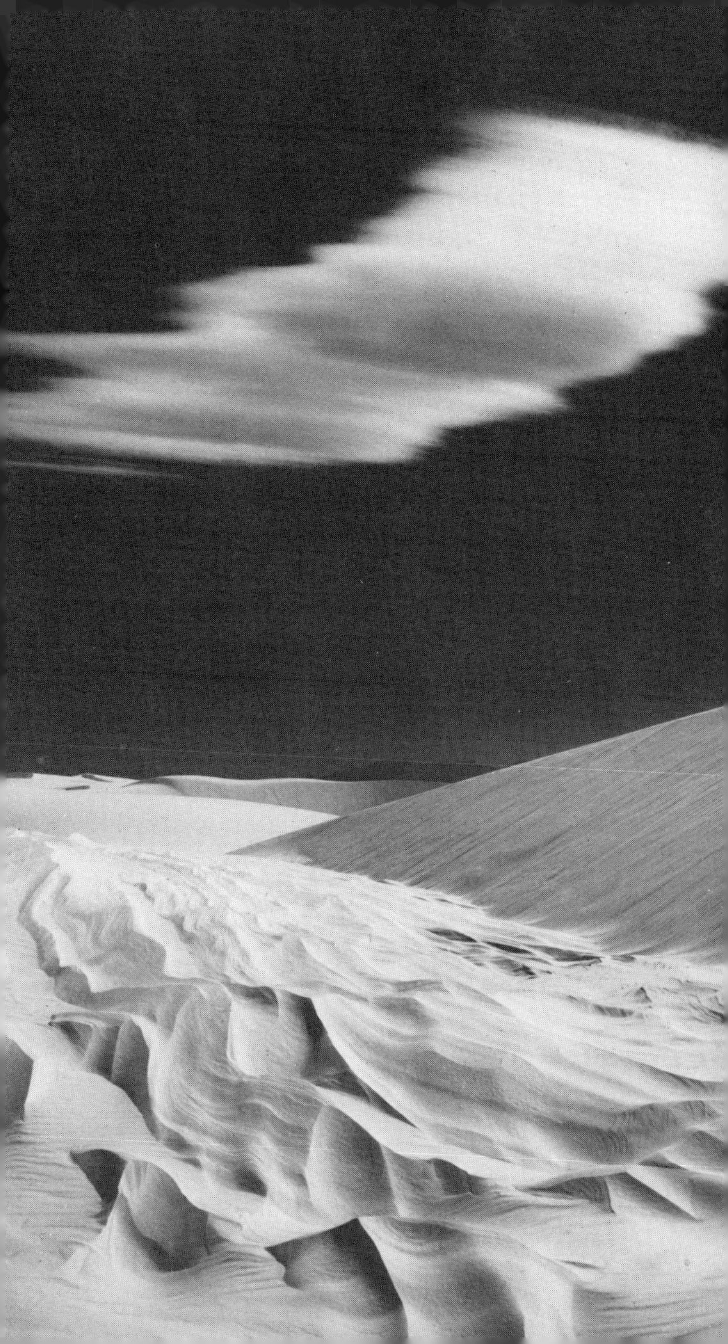

How to Get Along with People

Many books and articles have been written on the problem of how to get along with people. Solomon, the wise man, zeroes in on an area that most writers forget—man's harmony with his Creator, God. Here's what he wrote: "When a man's ways please the Lord, he maketh even his enemies to be at peace with him" (Prov. 16:7).

In other words, Solomon is saying, that if you learn how to get along with God, the Lord will show you how to get along with others.

Jesus taught that the greatest commandment is, "Love the Lord thy God with all thy heart . . . " (Matt. 22:37). The next greatest commandment is, "Love thy neighbor as thyself" (Matt. 22:39).

Today, concentrate on your relationships with God. Then notice how his love and peace will help you with your relationships with others.

What Should a Christian's Attitude Be in Times Like These?

When Jesus was on earth, he stated, "All power is given unto me in heaven and in earth" (Matt. 28:18). He has the power to control the supply to all our needs — physical, emotional and spiritual.

"Be of good cheer," Jesus commanded, "I have overcome the world" (John 16:33). His lifestyle proved this truth. His complete trust was in the greatness and the goodness of his Father in heaven. Without the benefit of a socially prominent family, without financial backing or political pull, He established the kingdom of God, working through a handful of dedicated men.

Nothing could stop his ministry; not criticism, not the failure of trusted followers, not the hatred of jealous enemies, not even death itself. As He moved in God's will, there was a solution to every need. A coin in a fish's mouth to pay the taxes. A banquet from a boy's meager lunch. A resting place for his crucified body in a rich man's tomb.

"I have overcome the world," He said. The world of his day did not defeat him. Therefore, the world of our day need not defeat us because Christ is in our hearts and he is "the hope of glory" (Col. 1:27).

Unemployment, shortages or inflation — we need not fear them if we know that *God is our source of supply.* "In him we live, and move, and have our being" (Acts 17:28).

The Psalmist said confidently, "The Lord is my shepherd; I shall not want" (Ps. 23:1). Late in life he gave further testimony to God's provisions. "I have been young, and now am old; yet have I not seen the righteous forsaken, nor his seed begging bread" (Ps. 37:25).

This same truth is restated in Matthew 6:33 when Jesus promises that if we seek "first the kingdom of God, and his righteousness," the necessary things of life will be added unto us.

God has no recession, no shortages. "The earth is the Lord's, and the fullness thereof; the world, and they that dwell therein" (Ps. 24:1).

We will, as humans, feel the pressures of the social world around us. But we need never despair. Rather, we can say as did one Christian in a crisis, "It sure will be interesting to see how God will get us out of this situation!"

Such a triumphant attitude can be ours if we will follow these scriptural guidelines: trust, moderation, and hope.

The attitude of trust — We must not put our total trust in ourselves or in others but rather in the one who made us — God Himself. Jesus said, "Have faith in God" (Mark 11:22). If our faith is completely in him, we will not be anxious about anything. Rather, we will be able to give thanks in everything, "for this is the will of God in Christ Jesus concerning you" (1 Thess. 5:18). God, not favorable circumstances, will be our source of lasting joy.

The attitude of moderation — the Apostle Paul wrote, "Let your moderation be known unto all men. The Lord is at hand" (Phil. 4:5). Our lifestyle should always reflect a middle-of-the-road attitude toward the things of time. We are pilgrims and strangers, not country gentlemen. Consequently, we must neither despise material things nor deify them. They are simply to be used.

The attitude of hope — the Written Word, the Bible, and the Living Word, Jesus Christ, must be our hope for time and eternity.

Let us therefore face today and tomorrow with a secure, positive attitude — the birthright of those who know personally the Living God. Why worry when he does have everything in his control?

The Gift of Laughter

"A good laugh is sunshine in a house."
Thackeray

One of God's delightful ways of making days brighter and burdens lighter is by enabling people to see the bright side, the funny side of life. Wasn't it Abraham Lincoln who said, "With the fearful strain that is on me night and day, if I did not laugh I should die"? And the wise man, Solomon, wrote, "A merry heart doeth good like a medicine" (Prov. 17:22).

Georgette Wolf, a gifted Milwaukee poetess, has captured the humor of the homemaker in the following poems:

Dilemma

I just do not know what to do.
I've thought the problem through and
    through.
I've weighed them all — the cons and
    pros
And counted up the yeas and nos.

I've sought advice from everywhere
For people really seem to care.
Still I cannot make up my mind
Which is the indecisive kind.

It's rather drastic after all
And once done, cannot be recalled.
I guess you'll think me silly but,
It is, you know, his first haircut.

Physical Fitness

My neighbor right across the street
Is jogging to keep down her weight.
My sister-in-law has joined a spa,
She has to leave the house by eight.
My best friend, Susan, swims a lot,
Unless, of course, the air's too cold.
What do I do to stay so trim?
Well — see — I have a two year old.

First Baby

I knew the child would be a girl,
My mother's instinct told me that
And I began to try out names
Like Anne and Melanie and Pat.

I thought how she would look like me,
A smaller version, but still true,
With dark brown hair and eyes that are
The family blend of green and blue.

And so the months passed swiftly by.
I think my time has come at last.
Please get my bag. No, I can walk.
Just promise me you won't drive fast.

Well, here I am, back in my room.
It really wasn't all that bad.
Now, have you seen them, our twin
    sons,
Who look exactly like their dad?

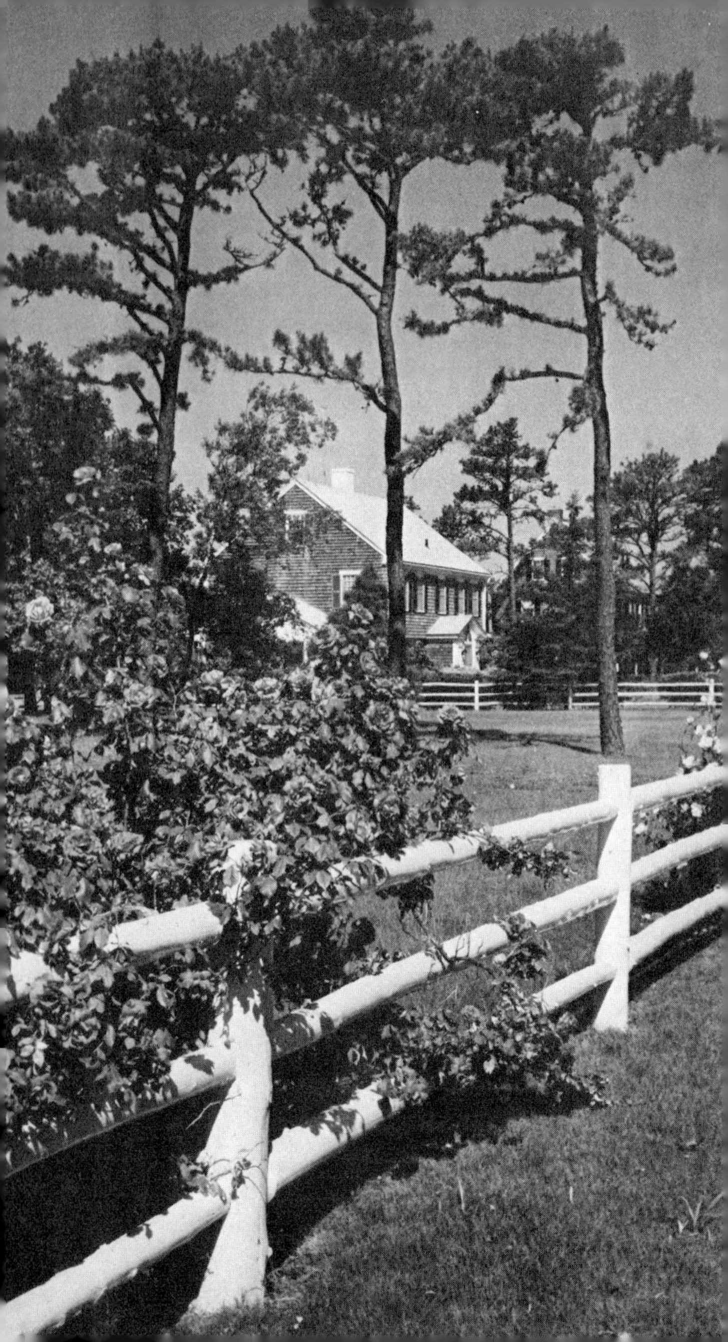

God's Prescription for Happy Homes

The following Bible verses outline attitudes and actions which bring happiness to the home:

"Honour thy father and thy mother: that thy days may be long upon the land which the Lord thy God giveth thee" (Exod. 20:12).

"A wise son maketh a glad father: but a foolish man despiseth his mother" (Prov. 15:20).

"Whoso findeth a wife findeth a good thing, and obtaineth favour of the Lord" (Prov. 18:22).

"Submitting yourselves one to another in the fear of God" (Eph. 5:21).

"Wives, submit yourselves unto your own husbands, as unto the Lord. For the husband is the head of the wife, even as Christ is the head of the church: and he is the saviour of the body" (Eph. 5:22-23).

"Husbands, love your wives, even as Christ also loved the church, and gave himself for it . . . so ought men to love their wives as their own bodies. He that loveth his wife loveth himself" (Eph. 5:25,28).

"Likewise, ye husbands, dwell with them according to knowledge, giving honour onto the wife, as unto the weaker vessel, and as being heirs together of the grace of life; that your prayers be not hindered" (1 Pet. 3:7).

"He that spareth his rod hateth his son: but he that loveth him chasteneth him betimes" (Prov. 13:24).

"Fathers, provoke not your children to wrath: but bring them up in the nurture and admonition of the Lord" (Eph. 6:4).

"Blessed are the peacemakers: for they shall be called the children of God" (Matt. 5:9).

"A soft answer turneth away wrath: but grievous words stir up anger" (Prov. 15:1).

I Give Thee Thanks

I give Thee thanks, my God and my Redeemer
For all the blessings which are mine today;
I give Thee thanks for food, for drink, for shelter.
For sleep each night, for work to do each day.
For health, for strength, for sight, for touch, for hearing.
For family, friends and all that I hold dear,
I give Thee thanks, conscious that all these blessings
Are mine today because Thou placed them here.

I give Thee thanks, my God and my Redeemer,
For all those things unseen by mortal eye,
For joy, for peace, for hope that springs eternal,
For mansions waiting me beyond the sky.
For all Thou art, my God and my Redeemer,
I give Thee thanks, as fall my joyful tears;
My heart is full with praise and love and worship
For all Thy blessings through the passing years.

Nat Olson

How to Know What to Do

"If you really want God's will and seek it, that is exactly what you'll get! Prayer without a commitment of the heart and will is an exercise in futility. Equally disastrous is the attitude of 'I want God's will, so whatever happens must be His will.'" So writes Dr. Robert A. Cook, president of King's College.

He continues, "It is the combination of desiring and seeking, obeying and believing, that gets results. The three verbs in Philippians 4:6-9 say it very well: 'Pray . . . think . . . do.' There is no substitute for the prayer that expresses the heart's desire, the thought that 'does its homework' and the obedience that does — right now — what one knows he ought to do . . . If your tomorrows are unclear, wait. A great servant of God once told me, 'If you don't know the will of God about a matter, it is because you don't need to know . . . yet.'"

The Healing Power of Forgiveness

After having met Corrie ten Boom in person, this author believes as never before that there *is* healing power in forgiveness.

Looking at her peaceful, joyous face, one can hardly imagine all the suffering she went through in that Nazi prison camp, as described in her book, *The Hiding Place.*

How can a woman in her eighties, having lost both father and sister through a murderous regime, not only survive but bless millions of people through her testimony? The answer is found in the word, forgiveness. Corrie has been willing to forgive the very men who caused the death of her father and sister. Forgiveness has freed her from self-pity, bitterness, and resentment.

Forgiveness will bring healing to anyone who is willing to let this power from God flow through him.

Jesus taught that we should pray, "Forgive us our debts, as we forgive our debtors" (Matt. 6:12). With these words, he showed that our forgiveness from God is proportionate to the forgiveness we show to others.

This brings us to the three dimensions of forgiveness.

First, we must forgive ourselves. Through prayer, we must eliminate our guilt, resentment, and bitterness. We must forgive ourselves for the sins and mistakes of the past. We must not let yesterday's shadows rob us of today's sunshine. "Forgetting those things which are behind," wrote the Apostle Paul (Phil. 3:13).

Secondly, we must forgive others. None of us can afford the luxury of continual resentment. "Let not the sun go down upon your wrath," says God's Word (Eph. 4:26). The hurts of life must be dealt with in the same manner as we deal with personal hygiene — on a daily basis.

Thirdly, we must forgive God. This seems to be a strange statement until we realize that all of us, at one time or another, have become angry with God and the things he allows to happen — sudden death, broken marriages, deformed children. We must learn to trust God when we cannot understand all his ways. We must confess our bitterness toward his dealings with the sons of men.

When we allow forgiveness in these three dimensions to flow through our minds and hearts, then, and only then, do we become total Christians.

If you find yourself unwilling to forgive someone, tell God your honest feelings. Then say, "But, Lord, I am willing to be *made* willing." He will give you the willingness to forgive and forget.

Develop the Attitude of Gratitude

"I don't have to thank anyone for anything I have," an old miser grumbled. "Everything I possess I got the hard way — by the sweat of my own brow."

"But who gave you the sweat?" asked his neighbor.

The old miser hung his head in guilty silence. He couldn't ignore the fact that God had given the sweat, the strength to work hard and gain material wealth.

Yes, everything we are or possess is because of God's loving kindness.

Mrs. Green thanked Tom, the grocery boy, for delivering a loaf of bread.

"Don't thank me. Thank Grocer Jones," Tom smiled. "He gave me the loaf to deliver."

But when she thanked the grocer, he said: "I get the bread from Baker Brown. He makes it. So he deserves the thanks."

So Mrs. Green thanked the baker. But he told her that Miller Milligan should be given her gratitude. "Without Milligan's flour, I couldn't make bread," Brown explained.

The miller told her to thank Farmer Foster because they made the flour from Foster's wheat. But the farmer also protested, "Don't thank me, thank God," Foster said. "If he didn't give my farm sunshine and rain, I couldn't grow wheat."

Yes, even a common loaf of bread can be traced back to the giver of all good gifts — God.

A housewife wrote:

Thank God for dirty dishes;
They have a tale to tell,
While others may go hungry,
We are eating well.
With home, health, and happiness,
I shouldn't want to fuss;
By the stack of evidence,
God's been very good to us.

The Bible says, "In everything give thanks" (1 Thess. 5:18). Therefore, practice the attitude of gratitude. Your thankfulness will bring you happiness. Try it — and see.

Feel Your Need of a Change?

Millions of people, camera in hand, loaded with fishing gear, or just traveling light, head for the seashore, the mountains, or a hundred and one other places. Their one common desire is *a change*.

Many are tired of their jobs, their environments, and themselves. A vacation in a quiet place seems to be the way out.

The Psalmist David felt his need to get away from it all. But soon he realized that the strength and the calmness he needed would not be found in escaping from his post of duty. He discovered that real soul rest does not come from *around* but from *above;* not just a new view, but a different viewpoint; not altitude, but attitude. He expressed it this way: "I will lift up mine eyes unto the hills, from whence cometh my help. My help cometh from the Lord, which made heaven and earth" (Ps. 121:1-2). David didn't look just *at* the hills; he looked *above* the hills to his helper and strength — God. In Him he found the restoration he needed.

Someone has pointed out that we often ask the Lord to change our circumstances, or other people, but seldom do we ask Him to change ourselves. God is interested in changing people. God has promised that "if any man be in Christ, he is a new creature: old things are passed away; behold, all things are become new" (2 Cor. 5:17).

Why not allow the Lord to change you through His love and power?

One Solitary Life

Author Unknown

Here is a man who was born in an obscure village, the child of a peasant woman. He grew up in another obscure village. He worked in a carpenter shop until He was thirty, and then for three years He was an itinerant preacher. He never wrote a book. He never held an office.

He never owned a home. He never set foot inside a big city. He never traveled two hundred miles from the place where He was born. He had no credentials but himself.

Nineteen wide centuries have come and gone and today He is the centerpiece of the human race and the leader of progress. I am far within the mark when I say that all the armies that ever marched, and all the navies that ever were built, and all the parliaments that ever sat, and all the kings that ever reigned, put together, have not affected the life of man upon this earth as powerfully as that One Solitary Life.

How to Pray More Effectively

The Bible is a book of prayer. It is the record of what happens when people commune with a prayer-hearing and prayer-answering God.

Tennyson wrote:
"More things are wrought by prayer than this world dreams of . . ."

Prayer Is Asking and Receiving

Jesus said, "Ask and it shall be given you . . ." (Luke 11:9). Bartimaeus asked for sight and received perfect vision. The Early Church prayed for Peter's release from prison and Peter was set free.

Right praying gets right answers! We expect water from a faucet. If no water comes out when we turn the faucet, we call the plumber. In other words, we expect results!

Yet much of the modern teaching on prayer gives the impression that we are "spiritually immature" if we always ask God for things. We are just to enjoy spiritual and emotional communion.

But Jesus taught otherwise. He told us to pray: "Give us this day our daily bread." He said if we ask for bread, we won't be given a stone. He taught us to expect good things from our Heavenly Father!

Prayer Is Not Overcoming God's Reluctance; It's Grabbing Hold of His Willingness

In Psalm 84, we read ". . . No good thing will He withhold from them that walk uprightly." Psalm 37:4 promises "Delight thyself also in the Lord; and He shall give thee the desires of thine heart." Jesus said that if human fathers love to give good gifts to their children, how much more will our Heavenly Father give the Holy Spirit to those who ask Him!

The Bible pictures God as loving and merciful, anxious to bless His children with good gifts. Therefore, let us put out of our minds the idea that we must beg and plead before we hope to get anything from the Lord. He is "more willing to give than we are to receive."

Prayer is Precious To God

What parent can resist the charm of his child's voice? It's music to a parent's ears. The Book of Revelation gives insight into how God feels about hearing from His children. "And when He had taken the book, the four beasts and four and twenty elders fell down before the Lamb, having every one of them harps, and golden vials full of odours, which are the prayers of the saints" (Rev. 5:8).

Prayer is fragrantly beautiful to the Lord! Revelation 8:3 says, "And another angel came and stood at the altar, having a golden censer; and there was given unto him much incense, that he should offer it with the prayers of all saints upon the golden altar which was before the throne." Then verse 4 adds, "And the smoke of the incense, which came with the prayers of the saints, ascended up before God out of the angel's hand."

After reading these descriptions, can we ever doubt that our prayers are vital to God? He loves to hear from us. He made us for communion with Him. So let us pray because this is the way to receive. Let us pray for He is willing to bless us. Let us pray because our prayers are precious to our Creator.

Perhaps you're asking, "If prayer is so simple — asking and receiving; prayer is not overcoming God's reluctance but grabbing hold of His willingness; if prayer is so fragrant to the Lord, why aren't my prayers answered?"

Some of the following hindrances may apply.

A lack of wholeheartedness: It is so easy to say a hurried prayer and feel that we have really prayed about a given matter. But Jeremiah 29:13 gives these words from Jehovah: "And ye shall seek me, and find me, when ye shall search for me with all your heart." God is worthy of our entire being getting involved in the prayer. Not just our lips but our heart as well, and our mind, and our will. Give yourself wholeheartedly to prayer and watch the answers come!

A lack of faith: James, in the first chapter of his epistle, verses 6 through 8, points out that a Christian must "ask" in faith, nothing wavering " . . . for he that wavereth is like a wave of the sea driven with the wind and tossed. For let not that man think that he shall receive anything of the Lord. A double minded man is unstable in all his ways."

In other words, you can get more of your prayers answered if you will stop doubting just because the answer didn't come air mail! Faith believes even when the senses say the opposite. Hebrews 11:1 states that "faith is the substance of things hoped for, the evidence of things not seen." Faith is tangible believing.

When you pray, do you really believe the answer is on the way? Or do you just hope that something might happen?

A lack of being specific: Jesus made it very clear when He said, "What things soever ye desire, when ye pray, believe that ye receive them, and ye shall have them" (Mark 11:24).

It is up to us to name the "what things." Bartimaeus asked for sight. The Centurion asked for the healing of his servant. The dying thief asked for a place in paradise.

If we are not specific, how will we know when God answers?

A lack of hatred for sin: The Psalmist David expressed this fact well when he wrote, "If I regard iniquity in my heart, the Lord will not hear me" (Ps. 66:18). "Regard" means to look at without doing anything to correct the situation.

God does not have to answer our prayers if we stubbornly refuse to forsake our sinning. Isaiah 59:1 and 2 states: "Behold, the Lord's hand is not shortened, that it cannot save; neither his ear heavy, that it cannot hear: But your iniquities have separated between you and your God, and your sins have hid His face from you, that He will not hear."

James 5:16 shows the importance of getting our relationship right if we want our prayers answered. "Confess your faults one to another, and pray for one another, that ye may be healed. The effectual fervent prayer of a righteous man availeth much."

Is there any sin that you are looking at without doing anything about?

A lack of knowing God's will: Many people pray for things that are not in God's will. They need to read and study God's Word in Christ. God's Word is God's will.

Jesus gave two requirements for getting prayer answered:

1) "If ye, abide in Me" — we have to be born into Christ's family.
2) "And My Words abide in you" — we have to be in regular study of His Word.

If these requirements are met, Jesus promises, ". . . ye shall ask what ye will, and it shall be done unto you" (John 15:7).

Get to know the Giver better and He will be able to give you more.

A lack of persistence: Man's basic flaw is impatience. To develop patience in us, the Lord allows us to wait for our answers. In the meantime, he expects us to "keep asking, keep knocking, keep seeking."

In Luke 11:1-13, where Jesus speaks about prayer, he tells the story of the man who gives his friend bread at midnight. The reason the man responds is because of his friend's "importunity" — fervent persistence.

God is persistent. He faithfully sends the rain on the just and the unjust. And little by little, more of the unjust become just. That's how God builds His kingdom — persistently! Why not determine now to begin an effective, persistent prayer life? Remember, God is "only a prayer away"!

Let God Talk to You

Could a loving God be a silent God? No. If you love someone, you want to communicate with them. Yet many people believe that a Supreme Being made this world ages ago and hasn't been heard from since.

The Bible, however, pictures God, not as some far-off potentate but as a loving Heavenly Father vitally concerned about the lives of His children now. Distance and time are no problems to God. He knows how to "get through." "God, who at sundry times and in divers manners spake in time past unto the fathers by the prophets, hath in these last days spoken unto us by His Son" (Heb. 1:1,2).

From Genesis to Revelation, we see God's various methods of communication.

Through Nature

Psalm 19:1 says, "The heavens declare the glory of God and the firmament showeth His handywork." Abraham Lincoln told a friend that he could not understand how any man could look at the stars and still be an atheist! Colossians 1:16,17 states that everything was created by the Lord Jesus and for Him, and "by Him all things consist" or are held together.

Through Conscience

Romans 2:15 describes the Gentiles as "their conscience also bearing witness and their thoughts the mean while accusing or else excusing one another." God-consciousness is in every man. Every man has inborn light (John 1:9). Every man has inborn faith (Rom. 12:3).

If we use the faith and the light we have, God will give us more.

Through the Written Word

"Put it in writing" is a rule of thumb in the business world. There is a permanency to the written word which no other media offers.

God wrote the Ten Commandments in tables of stone (Exod. 20). The words of the prophets of God were put in writing. Jesus Himself said to the unbelieving Jewish leaders, "For had ye believed Moses, ye would have believed me: for he wrote of me. But if ye believe not his writings, how shall ye believe my words?" (John 5:46,47).

The question is asked: "But how do we know that our Bible today is even near the meaning of the original manuscripts?"

At least two good reasons stand out for confidence in our present-day Bible:

First, the King James Version or Authorized Version of 1611 is the result of careful study of the Hebrew and Greek texts by forty-seven scholars under the authorization of King James I of England. For over three centuries, it has held first place in the hearts of believers throughout the English-speaking world.

Second, the Dead Sea Scrolls, discovered in the spring of 1947 in the caves of the Judean Wilderness, west of the Dead Sea, are at least 1,000 years older than any previously discovered Old Testament manuscripts. There are manuscripts or fragments of manuscripts for every one of the Old Testament's thirty-nine books, except Esther. The largest and best preserved of all the scrolls is the Scroll of Isaiah. Recognized as the oldest Hebrew manuscript of any book in the Bible, it basically agrees with the Hebrew texts used in the King James translation.

Add to these two good reasons the prophetic Scripture in our Bible that is being fulfilled before our eyes, and you will see why we can trust the Bible.

Through the Voice of the Prophets

E. M. Bounds says, "Men are God's methods."

Whenever God wanted to speak dramatically to His people, He would raise up a prophet — an Ezekiel, a Jeremiah, a Hosea — someone who would proclaim his message in a unique way.

Contrary to popular thinking, a prophet does not necessarily have to be "a foreteller." But he is always a "forth-teller" — speaking the Word of God whether or not the people want to hear.

The Prophets of God were anointed men. Second Peter 1:21 describes them as "holy men of God [who] spake as they were moved by the Holy Ghost."

Between Malachi and Matthew there is no record of any voice being raised for God. After these "400 Silent Years," God decided to communicate once more to man. And this time He used . . .

The Living Word;

He had used nature, conscience, the written word, and the preaching of the prophets. But now, He was sending "The Logos," the Word, in the Person of His Son, Jesus Christ. "And the Word was made flesh and dwelt among us, (and we beheld His glory, the glory as of the only begotten of the Father,) full of grace and truth" (John 1:14).

God had told Moses to tell the people that the great "I Am" had sent him to lead them out of Egypt. Now Jesus, "the Living Word," finished the sentence: "I am the way, the truth, and the life."

Through Laws Written on the Heart

The children of Israel demonstrated man's inability to obey written laws. Before Moses could return with the Ten Commandments, his people were caught up in a frenzied, pagan dance around a golden calf!

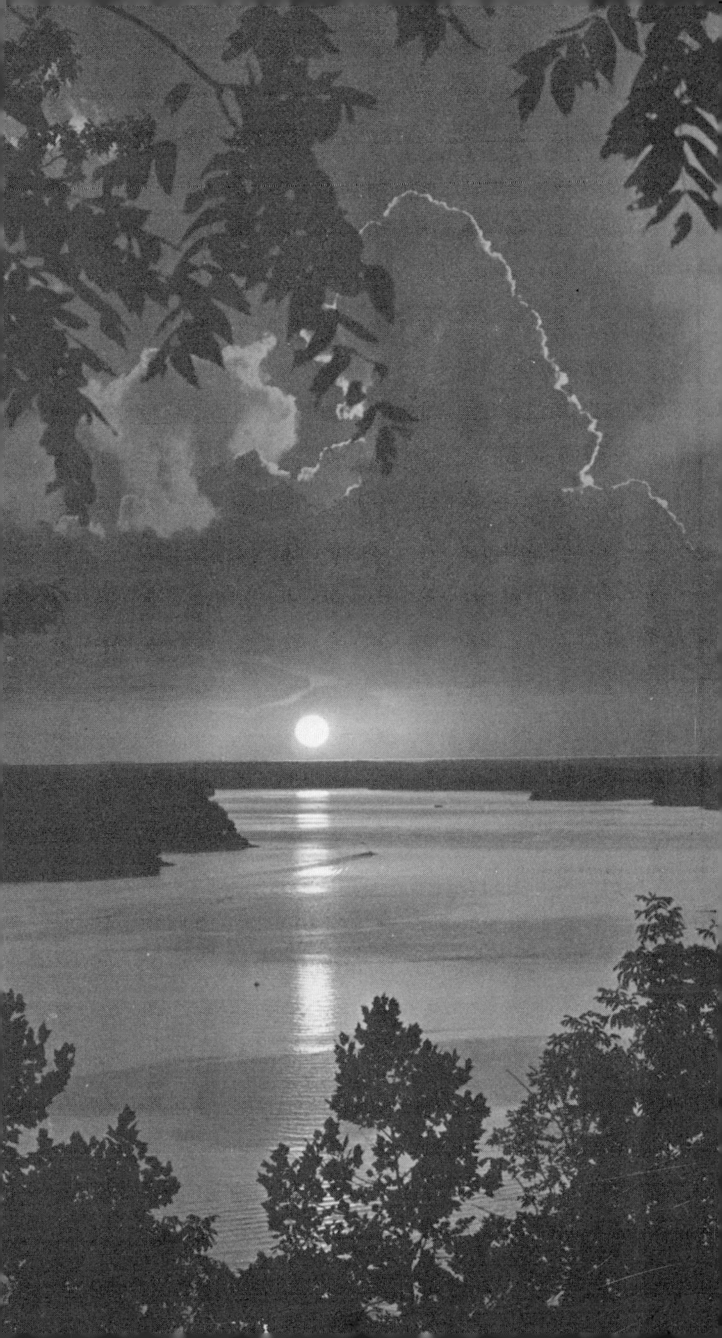

Jesus Christ taught His disciples to worship "in spirit and in truth" . . . to love and act because of the law written in their hearts by the Holy Spirit. The Holy Spirit, residing in our hearts, is the only way to prevent further inconsistencies in our lives! No one has a list long enough to include all the DO's and DON'Ts of the Christian life-style. When God's laws are in our hearts, however, we will be careful to do everything for God's glory, and for the good of others. We will be cured of "I" trouble!

"For this is the covenant that I will make with the house of Israel after those days, saith the Lord; I will put My laws into their mind, and write them in their hearts, and I will be to them a God, and they shall be to me a people" (Heb. 8:10).

Through Living Epistles — Changed Lives!

Someone has called this means of communication, "The Gospel in shoe leather."

Another has termed it, "The Gospel according to *you.*"

Writing to the Christians at Corinth, the Apostle Paul described them as "our epistle . . . known and read of all men" (2 Cor. 3:2). He knew their lives were being read even by those who would never read the Word of God.

Jesus returned to God the Father so that the Holy Spirit might be outpoured — not just in Christ's one life — but in the lives of believers everywhere. ". . . greater works than these shall he do; because I go unto my father," said Jesus (John 14:12).

You and I are a part of God's final communication program to this age. What is the Gospel according to YOU?

God has spoken! God is *speaking!* Are we listening?

Walk in the Light

In Cliff Dudley's introduction to the book, *Bought and Paid For,* the shocking yet true story of Don and Joanie Larson, he writes: "Ofttimes I'm afraid that we have grown accustomed to the darkness and it sometimes takes the contrast for us to appreciate the light . . . This book tells the real life story of two people caught up in pride and self-indulgence to the extent of near destruction and how the Word of God cuts through the difficulties of life . . . God's power, forgiveness and deliverance is greater than any sin, situation, or any power of darkness."

The Bible, in 1 John 1:7, verifies the preceding paragraph: "If we walk in the light, as he [Christ] is in the light, we have fellowship one with another, and the blood of Jesus Christ his son cleanseth us from all sin."

There is help and hope for us each day if we are willing to walk in the light of God's Word.

God Created the Material World

It is unfortunate that many people feel God is interested only in our spiritual well-being. The Bible, however, shows that God created the material world. Nowhere does the Bible condemn the material things of life. The finger of warning is pointed at man's attitude toward these things. First Timothy 6:10 says, ". . . the love of money is the root of all evil . . . " Jesus taught, ". . . how hard is it for them that trust in riches to enter into the kingdom of God" (Mark 10:24). God is concerned that the emotions of love and trust be focused on the Creator, not on created things. Materialism is idolatry.

Shortages remind us of our dependence on God — the Lord of both the spiritual and material kingdoms.

Good News for Bad Hearts

In 1785 William Withering, a medical doctor from England, gave a dried portion of the foxglove leaf to a patient whose heart was beating too rapidly. The doctor was thrilled to see his patient's heartbeat slow to a normal pulse in a very short time.

Dr. Withering's discovery was destined to eventually save the lives of millions of heart patients around the world. The most popular medication extracted from the foxglove leaf is digitoxin which slows the heartbeat down to a normal rate and causes the heart muscle to become stronger.

God, who put the amazing foxglove flower on planet earth also sent his Son to earth to give the remedy of spiritual heart trouble. In John 14:1,6,7 Jesus said, "Let not your heart be troubled: Ye believe in God, believe also in me . . . I am the way, the truth, and the life: no man cometh unto the Father but by me."

Faith in Christ as personal Savior and Lord does cure the anxiety and guilt of the human heart.

"There is no fear in love, but perfect love casteth out fear: because fear hath torment" (1 John 4:18).

The Sun, The Moon

God, the Author of light, desires for people not to live in darkness, either physically or spiritually.

On the fourth day of creation, God put the sun in the heavens. Genesis 1:16 describes it as "the greater light to rule the day." Scientists tell us that the sun is the largest and the brightest of the stars visible to the naked eye, although it ranks among the smallest and the faintest of all the stars in the universe. The reason it appears so big and bright is because of its proximity to our planet, only ninety-three million miles away. The next nearest star is almost 300,000 times as far removed!

Inspired by the light from the sun and the light of God's love, John Keble wrote:

Sun of my soul! Thou Savior dear,
It is not night if Thou be near;
Oh, may no earthborn cloud arise
To hide Thee from Thy servant's eyes!

God never leaves anything half done. On the same day He created the sun to rule the day, He fashioned the moon, "the lesser light to rule the night" (Gen. 1:16).

Scientists verify that the moon is the lesser of the two. In fact, the sun gives off about 465,000 times more light than the moon. Yet, the moon has fascinated man throughout history. It has been credited with many claims that science now holds false. Only one major belief about the moon has borne the test of time and science — the movement of the ocean's tides is directly affected by the moon.

God Bless America

Some years ago, Carlos P. Romulo, the great Philippine patriot and one-time president of the UN General Assembly, said, on leaving America for his homeland: "I am going home, America — farewell. For seventeen years, I have enjoyed your hospitality, visited every one of your fifty states. I can say I know you well. I admire and love America. It is my second home. What I have to say now in parting is both a tribute and a warning. Never forget, Americans, that yours is a spiritual country. Yes,

I know that you are a practical people. Like others, I have marveled at your factories, your skyscrapers and your arsenals. But underlying everything else is the fact that America began as a God-loving, God-fearing, God-worshiping people, knowing that there is a spark of the divine in each one of us. It is this respect for the dignity of the human spirit which makes America invincible. May it always endure.

"And so I say again in parting, thank you, America, and farewell. May God keep you always — and may you always keep God."

This great soldier-statesman, who served with General Douglas MacArthur in World War II, analyzed America well. It is her spiritual resources which have made her rich and great. Only a continuance of these qualities will assure her continued greatness.

Breathing? Then Praise the Lord!

Psalm 150:6, concludes the Book of Psalms with this grand finale: "Let every thing that hath breath praise the Lord. Praise ye the Lord."

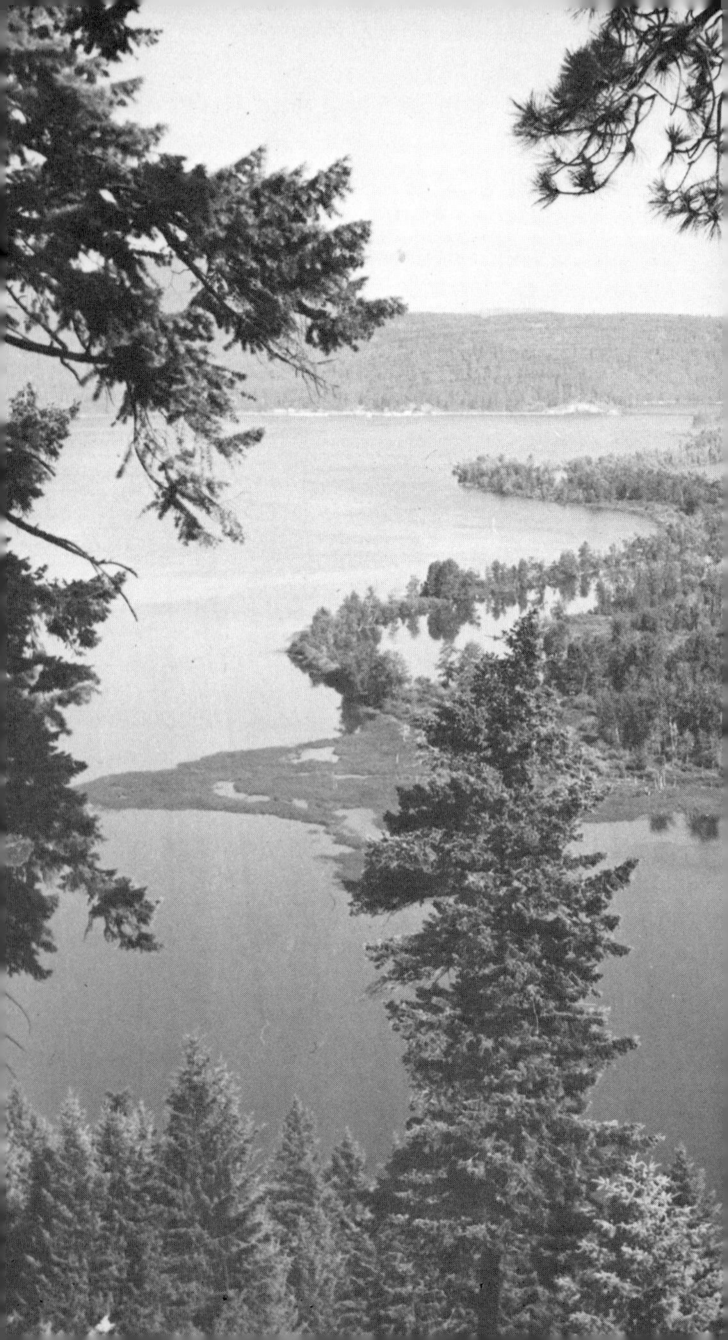

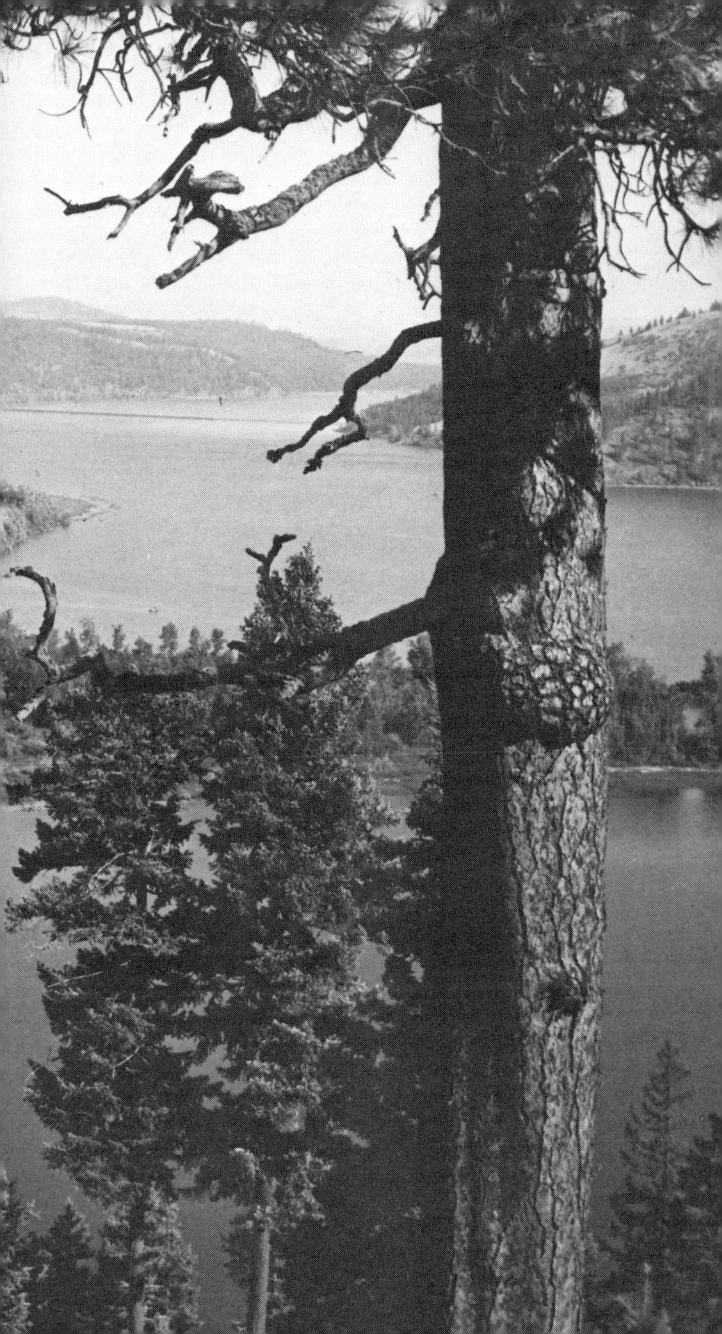

Air

Because of air pollution, we have become increasingly aware of how vital the thin layer of air which surrounds the earth is. Obviously, human life could not exist if God did not graciously provide air — composed of oxygen, nitrogen, and minute mixtures of other gases.

If oxygen were the only element present, our earth would go up in flames. (Oxygen is the gas that causes substances to burn.) If nitrogen were the only element in the air, nothing would burn. It extinguishes a flame quickly. If only nitrogen and oxygen were present, no plants could adequately grow. Plants must have carbon dioxide, yet this gas will not support animal life. God, however, mixed carbon dioxide in amounts that would not harm man yet permit plants to get adequate amounts for growth. Who but an all-wise Creator could mix oxygen, nitrogen, carbon dioxide, and other gases making earth a safe place for man, animals, and plants?

The Apostle Paul taught that God "giveth to all life, and breath, and all things. For in him we live, and move, and have our being" (Acts 17:25,28).

Our very breath is provided through the mercy of our Heavenly Father!

Light and Color

Light is so vital to life that the first act of God in creation was to say, "Let there be light" (Gen. 1:3).

Without light, the chlorophyll of the leaf would not function. Without light, plants, animals, and man would starve. Our very existence is dependent upon ". . . the Father of lights, with whom is no variableness, neither shadow of turning" (James 1:17).

Without light, we could not enjoy the beauty of earth and sky for we see only the light which is reflected. When light is absent we see nothing.

Jesus, well aware of the natural world He and the Father created, said: "I am the light of the world: he that followeth me shall not walk in darkness, but shall have the light of life" (John 8:12).

On another occasion, He told his followers, "You are the light of the world." In Matthew 5:16, He commanded, "Let your light so shine before men, that they may see your good works, and glorify your Father which is in heaven."

One of Christ's later followers, Sir Isaac Newton, began a series of experiments to investigate the nature of color and its association with light. God inspired him to place a prism in a beam of sunlight shining through a small hole in a shutter of a darkened room. Newton discovered that the beam of light produced the colors of the spectrum — red, orange, yellow, green, blue, and violet. Later, using a second prism, the young scientist found the colors recombined and produced a white light. He then knew that light — white to the eye — was, in reality, a combination of all colors of the spectrum.

No Shortages with God

In this time of oil, power, and food shortages, the Bible speaks out with the comforting message of God's ability to meet any lack of man, spiritual or material.

In the Old Testament, the children of Israel felt "the crunch" on many occasions. One time, it was the lack of meat in their all-manna diet. God became weary of their complaining and deluged them with more quail than they could comfortably eat (Exod. 16:13). On another occasion, there was a water shortage. God told Moses to strike a rock and out of it flowed cool, refreshing water (Num. 20:11). For forty years, God met every need of these people as they wandered in the wilderness. He sent a pillar of fire to guide them by night and a cloud to protect them from the burning sun by day (Exod. 40:38).

Why Shortages Come

If God has an abundance of everything man needs, why do shortages plague the human race? The Bible teaches that material shortages come when people violate spiritual laws.

The Old Testament prophet Malachi, in chapter 3, tells God's people they are suffering material want because they have robbed God "of tithes and offerings." He assures them that their economy will change for the better *if* they will obey Jehovah by bringing all their tithes into the storehouse. God said, ". . . I will not open you the windows of heaven and pour you out a blessing, that there shall not be room enough to receive it" (Mal. 3:10).

The New Testament story of the Prodigal Son is a story of a father's forgiveness and love for his wayward boy. It also illustrates how material shortages can be met. Away from his loving father, the young rebel ran out of money and food. Finally, the hunger pangs awakened his memories of abundant supply at his father's house. He returned home and found his material and spiritual needs amply met (Luke 15).

Could today's shortages be God's way of reminding a prodigal generation that it's high time it returned home to the Heavenly Father? Perhaps He is taking away material "privileges" to teach his disobedient creation vital spiritual lessons.

"He that loveth his brother abideth in the light" (1 John 2:10).

"Christ has turned all our sunsets into sunrise!"
>   Clement of Alexandria

The Solution to Shortages

When shortages do come, we should remember Christ's words to His worried followers: ". . . be of good cheer; I have overcome the world" (John 16:33). Jesus took the problems of life in stride. He manifested no bitterness because of the meager circumstances of His childhood. He did not rebel at the heavy Roman taxation. ". . . render therefore unto Caesar the things which are Caesar's; and unto God the things that are God's" (Matt. 22:21). When he preached to the hungry multitude, he took the lunch of a boy, blessed it, and performed a miracle of multiplication that fed over 5,000 people.

In the Sermon on the Mount, Jesus told the crowd not to worry about food, drink, and clothes because that is the concern of people who do not know the living God. In Matthew 6:33, he says, in essence: "If you would be concerned about anything, let it be about the kingdom of God. That's worth your emotional concern. Make God's kingdom number one and your Father will give you the necessities of life."

LIGHT FOR YOUR FUTURE

" . . . the path of the just
is as the shining light,
that shineth more and
more unto the perfect day."

(Prov. 4:18)

"The Future Is As Bright As The Promises of God"

General Douglas MacArthur, on his seventy-fifth birthday, made this thought-packed observation of age:

"Youth is not entirely a time of life; it is a state of mind. It is not wholly a matter of ripe cheeks, red lips, or supple knees. It is a temper of the will, a quality of the imagination, a vigor of the emotions . . . nobody grows old by merely living a number of years. People grow old only by deserting their ideals.

"You are as young as your faith, as old as your doubt; as young as your self-confidence, as old as your fear; as young as your hope, as old as your despair.

"In the central place of every heart there is a recording chamber. So long as it receives a message of beauty, hope, cheer, and courage — so long are you young. When the wires are all down and your heart is covered with the snow of pessimism and the ice of cynicism, then, and only then, are you grown old."

Another great leader, King David, voiced his outlook on life in Psalm 37:25: "I have been young, and now am old; yet have I not seen the righteous forsaken, nor his seed begging bread."

All Good Things Do Not Come To An End

William Jennings Bryan, famous orator and three-time nominee for the Presidency of the United States said:

"Christ gave us proof of immortality. And yet it would hardly seem necessary that one should rise from the dead to convince us that the grave is not the end.

"To every created thing God has given a tongue that proclaims a resurrection. If the Father deigns to touch with divine power the cold and pulseless heart of the buried acorn and make it burst forth from its prison walls, will he leave neglected in the earth the soul of man, made in the image of his Creator?

"If he stoops to give the rosebush, whose withered blossoms float upon the autumn breeze, the sweet assurance of another springtime, will he refuse the world of hope to the sons of men when the frost of another winter comes? If matter, mute and inanimate, though changed by force of nature into a multitude of forms, can never die, will the spirit of man suffer annihilation when it has paid a brief visit, like a royal guest, to the tenement of clay? No. I am as sure that there is another life as I am that I live today."

The Best Is Yet To Come

Alice Hansche Mortenson

Even in advancing years,
    I still find life exciting.
I yield to Him all anxious fears —
    The future is inviting.
Each day I live God seems to grant
    Some special, sweet surprise,
As miracles of grace unfold
    Before my very eyes!

So it's become a habit now,
    To eagerly await,
The moving of His loving hand
    To open up some gate
Of service, never dreamed before,
    And so there's no regret
O'er disappointments of the past —
    The best is coming yet!

However, should His plan for me
    Include inactive days
Before He takes me to himself,
    May it be for His praise.
So I'll not fear, but joyfully
    Look t'ward the setting sun,
Assured that in my Father's house
    The best is yet to come.

THE BEST IS YET TO COME by Alice Hansche Mortenson. Copyright 1977.
Reprinted by permission of Beacon Hill Press, Kansas City, Missouri.

Vaya con Dios!

We can think of no better way to close this book than with the beautiful expression used by our Spanish-speaking friends: "Vaya con Dios!"

It simply means: "Go with God!"

Yes, go with God. Don't try to face today's problems with your own strength. Let His strength flow through you.

Go with God! Don't face the uncertain tomorrows of this topsy-turvy world with your own wisdom. Rest your case in the comforting truth that although you do not know what the future holds, you do know the One Who holds the future. With Him in control, what is there to fear?

Make no room for the dark uncertainties most people dread. You now know the truth, and the truth has set you free. Your light has come!